AF342374

POSSESSIONS
poems by Hale Chatfield

Cleveland State University Poetry Center
Cleveland Poets Series No. 36

ACKNOWLEDGMENTS

Grateful acknowledgment is made to the publications listed below, in which the following poems have previously appeared:

"The Confession of Thomas Owl," *Chowder Review* #7 (1976).

"The Flesh" (originally, "I Got Back Exhausted") and "Another Love Poem," both from *73 Ohio Poets, Cornfield Review* (1978).

"Woman at a Window," *Big Moon* I:3 (1975).

"Abelard to Heloise," *Attention Please* I:3 (1976).

"Contretemps," *Midatlantic Review* #2 (1975).

"Tears" and "The Life of Lovers," both from *Poetry Now* .

"Rain Coming Maybe" and "Ruby Church," both from *Northeast* .

"George," "The Fears of Running Bear," and "All Angels Are Terrible," all from *What Color Are Your Eyes?* Copyright 1978 by Hale Chatfield.

"Scherzo," *Agni Review* #5/6 (1976).

"The Passionate Shepherd to his Love," *Pigiron* (1977).

"Going to Work for Horace Sondergard," *Dacotah Territory* #14 (1977).

Cover picture by George Schroeder.

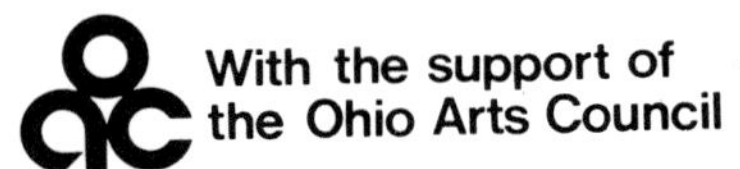

for Denise and our children
and for all creatures

CONTENTS

*By our Apostolic authority
we define and proclaim that
the Indians, or any other
peoples who may be hereafter
discovered by Catholics,
although they be not Christian,
must in no way be deprived
of their liberty or their possessions.*

Pope Paul III
1537

THE CONFESSION OF THOMAS OWL

I have tried
to feel sorry.

Contrition requires
effort, but the
effort itself is not
enough.

> Think of this: a raccoon
> is caught by its foot
> in the jaws of a trap.

I see.

> The trap was set
> for a muskrat. The
> raccoon is of course
> not a muskrat.

Yet surely
that is neither
the fault of the raccoon
nor the fault of the muskrat
for which the trap was intended.

And the man who set the trap?

> He is pleased: the raccoon
> is more valuable than
> the muskrat;
>
> at the same time
> he is very sad;
> life is so unpredictable.

Yet that is a sadness
outside of oneself: it is not guilt.
The sky is blue
and the weather benign.

Confession is meaningless
without contrition:

> the man confesses
> to the raccoon: "Raccoon
> I am sorry to have caught
> you this day."

> Yet he is not contrite.

I think I know him: he is
an Indian named
Thomas Owl.

> And he is not contrite.
> The raccoon listens to
> the man and feels the
> terrible pain. They are
> beside a small river:
> a creek.

The more one confesses
without being truly contrite,
the harder his heart becomes:
eventually it turns to stone.

> In the creekbed are many
> such hearts, small rounded
> stones the sizes of human fists:
> children's, women's, men's.
> The cold water bubbles over them.

Its voice says
kindness;

It says
I confess.

> Thomas Owl
> can feel what it must be like
> to be the raccoon.
>
> There are stones in the creekbed
> the sizes of the hearts
> of raccoons and muskrats.

It is not the same.
It cannot be the same.

> That is what Thomas Owl
> tells you one day in front

of the store:

> when he smiles
> his eyes wrinkle:
>
> he says, "It is not
> the same."

THE FLESH
(to be read twice in succession)

I got back exhausted
and sat down and poured myself some wine.
I thought, Maybe I ought to write her a letter
saying "I did that for you; I even
did *that* for you." And then I thought,
What's the use? She knows. She was nailing
us up with kisses in the kitchen, and all
the time that kid was out there,
and it was getting harder and harder to breathe.

I poured some more wine
and decided that in fact
I *would* write you something.
Even now you are reading it.
You read: the cross was an instrument
in wide use for the purpose of executing
criminals found guilty of a variety of
crimes ranging from theft to treason.
You read: it killed by suffocation,
as the weakening victim drowned
in his own weight, and you are finding it
harder and harder to breathe.

The boy knew, you said.
He didn't look like he knew much,
but I took him out and shot him anyway.
For you. He didn't look like he knew much
when I buried him, either. But he knew enough
by then I guess. I thought maybe I'd write
asking, "Are you *sure* ?" — but I should
have asked that a long time ago,

before there was anything to know:
before you took me in your arms
and kissed me as I reached for a piece of paper
to write all of this, and began it:
I got back exhausted.

WOMAN AT A WINDOW

Possibly you think
we can get out of this
alive:

        I have no time for that sort
of naiveté: look who
is here in this building with us:
Schlemmer the baker,
Martha with her two hats
which she wears on alternate days
as faithfully as St. Augustine,
in middle age, might have attended
his own tears;
oh the whole many of them!
none has left
alive, except
for those meaningless little
                excursions by which
                life is *defined:*
                        a visit to the library
                        a vacation at the seashore or in the moun-
                        tains
                        a need for contraceptives or groceries
                        a quest for a few flowers
                        and of course labor,
                                the getting of money;
these are hardly journeys,
certainly not escapes,
evasions, disappearances:

they come back inevitably,
almost always with something in their hands:
a dreary looking package,

a limp paper bag,
an umbrella, a folded newspaper,
a reticule (it is so boring
I could weep here at the window
watching them come back—

I could drive my hands through
the glass; I could shriek.
Poor creatures. They
would look up at my window
as if I had interrupted a dream:
they would see a black square of window,
a white, distant face— and wonder
was it a reflection?
a glitter of doves?).

> But of course Jesse did get away.
>   Before you came
> to be with me here in
> this room. The wallpaper
> was new then, yet it was
> even at that not very
> pretty.
>
> Once while we were making
> love I burst into tears
> and he said I looked
> like a monkey. He was
> not smiling; he merely
> looked at my face; he said
> it quite simply. And it is true.

These are the things
you fail to take into consideration
when you begin a sentence with
"I hope."

I cannot believe that a man
who lives this kind of life
does not sometimes
dream he is falling.

> Jesse used to dream
> he was falling: he
> would snap up in bed
> and scream. Very loud.
> Sometimes off and on
> for hours, sitting up
> in the dark, he would
> scream until the globe
> on that overhead lamp
> would begin to resonate.
>
> And all the while,
> gentle as a kitten,
> his one hand would
> purr along my thigh.

ABELARD TO HELOISE

"What shall we do:
having given up on grace, shall we
sit here and become incredibly rich?

"We shall have to sit very well
in that case; the pay
is not high

        —even when, as you do,
        you sit in precisely *that* way.
        it is worth a great deal
        to me.
        possibly to others.
        but money? I think not.

"And as for myself,
I *am* collecting things as I sit here:
thoughts which are merely beautiful
or ugly, plans
which I cannot enact from this chair,
dreams hopeless to reassemble.

        So you see
        we shall have to move
        or remain very poor."

CONTRETEMPS

If it is not under the rose
(I will speak candidly),
if there is nothing wrong at my house,
if it is not a case of "after this,
therefore *because of* this,"

yet still there are those
who will say, affecting tongues,
"sub rosa";
or *"chez vous"*;
or even, incredibly, *"post hoc*
ergo propter hoc."

They are great talkers
who use a foreign phrase
and then translate it for you—
for example, one will say:
> *"Was ich nicht weiss*
> *macht mich nicht heiss,*
> What I don't know
> doesn't make me hot."

As if we, the listeners, are
perfect imbeciles.

Furthermore, it is hot
under the roses at my house
after this and indeed
because of this.

And you *know* it.
It was your fucking idea.

GETTING ALONG ON LESS

If it keeps on like this
I don't know what I'll do.

> I don't either: maybe
> we should sell the fish
> or cut down on children.

We spend a great deal
on wishing we had more time
to ourselves . . .

> God yes: just to
> talk—
>
> we could stop that
> altogether.

The talk
and the occasional
intimacy.

> Yes, and the wishing
> we had time for them.

TEARS

In this poem
no one is weeping.

Not the lost child,
the new widow,
the old man who has come to nothing.

The girl who has surrendered easily
something of herself she had thought
immeasurably precious
regards in her mirror
a face as dry as paper.

The parched breeze
cannot drink at the eye
of the remorseful tyrant
or the humbled surgeon.

Notice how even the lonely
do not stipple this page
with the watermarks
of despair.

Surely I myself am not weeping.
I am fully absorbed by this dry poem
as I concentrate on the task
of bringing it to a close.

RAIN COMING MAYBE

The lights are growing visible
again, one by one,
in the fucking sky,
Marston says, looking at Venus
and a couple of stars.

Gomez once told me
Marston is half nuts. They don't
trust him much. Gomez said, the son
of a bitch is supposed to be an Apache
and he has those goddamned blue
eyes.

The eyes are indeed surprising;
right now they are precisely the color
of the sky Marston is looking at,
and you get a little spooked. You try
not to pay any attention. I poke
at the fire with my knife.

But then Marston says, Well it's going
to get dark pretty soon; the sun
has fallen way the hell down into the Pacific.
And then he says to Gomez,
You believe in the Pacific Ocean, macho?

Gomez says Fuck off. You watch
the jeep and make sure nobody
steals it. Do something useful.

Marston chuckles. Well it is a long way off
anyway, brother. A long way. He wets
his finger, picks up a few grains of sand

and rubs them over his teeth.
He spits.

Gomez says to me privately
Jesus Christ.

* * *

I think they are afraid of him
or they surely would have killed him
after the thing with Ewing's sister.

They followed him for three days
and when they caught up with him
he was rolling a cigarette
and just watching them come down at him
over the ridge.

All four of them had their carbines
pointed right at his nose. He said,
You look silly as hell. He said, This
is America, boys. Sit down and have
a smoke.

* * *

It's getting dark. Marston squats
next to me looking into the fire.
I am thinking about those blue eyes.
Marston nudges me with his elbow.
He says, Once I run into a nigger
who could speak Latin.

THE LIFE LOVERS

"When you are a child
on vacation with your family
you make friends:
important and sudden
friendships which are freedom
and privacy and the beginning
of a just death—the beginning of getting away,
of growing into the sunlight
and the fields of air.

"In Maine I met a girl
years ago wild and harmless as a fern.
She knew the woods, her father's farm,
the dusty balsam-smelling roads,
and the icy little rivers where
we would strip off our clothes
and swim the electric cold.
Shameless as any boy she would
sometimes step naked among the trees
and pee standing upright: alarming,
accurate, neat as peeled birch.
I did not then know the name
of the excitement she gave me,
and I have forgotten the name of the girl.

"She could have been named
Magic or Miracle or even Mary
and it would have made no difference
to me: she could climb
the steam of my breath, gather owls
peacefully on her shoulders and glide
with the chicken hawks over her father's fields;
the raucous crows she taught
first silence, then speech:

'Madonna,' they called her,
and wept when she left them
for home or for me.

"Now, these many years later,
I sometimes go to my window
late in the night and see her there
in the moonlight on the dew-moistened lawn;
she is fuller, a woman, but I know it is she—
breasts globed and luminous in the cool light,
a silver laciness where her legs and abdomen
conspire. I am naked, too, at my window:
the wood and glass do not keep me from her
as I dream my way over the lawn
to embrace her, and I find her as real
as the train throbbing in the valley;
or hickory smoke; or smooth skin.

"I do not know the name of my excitement
as our bodies touch, though surely
we have each known bodies enough
over the years. We raise our hands
above our heads, palm against palm,
as if, upright, innocently conjoined,
we are preparing to dive skyward into the stars.

"We grow out of our bodies
and out of our little lives:
gentle death takes us together
into what we have earned,
and the Milky Way, as we enter it
with a shudder of white sparks,
is a cold river."

GEORGE

I got sick of not fighting
and of believing that Indians
can't hold their liquor, George
said, and so now I get drunk
almost every night and about once
a week I fight like a son of a bitch.

* * *

George is a Pueblo
and he's a long way from home,
but he came here because at least there's Indians,
more or less. There are lots of kinds of Pueblos
and there always were.

I remember when Crow Feather first
found out George was moving in with us
and he went over to look. When he came
back he said Short ain't he, and ugly
as owlshit.

That's a pretty good picture of George,
but he's strong. And sometimes he's funny.

Once some white people
got into a wreck out on route nine
and were both pinned somehow
under their car. Everybody was standing
around trying to figure out what to do,
even the trooper.

So George went over and lifted up
one end of the car, and the people
crawled out in pretty good shape.

George told them You smell like booze.
Crazy bastards—I should have just let
you die.

>The trooper said That's pretty heavy talk
>ain't it chief? and George says
>in this phoney deep voice: *Ugh. Heap heavy.*
>*You betchum.* And then he says,
>normal, Look cop you keep off my ass
>or I'll catch 'em and put 'em back
>under the car.

ANOTHER LOVE POEM

The cells of skin are perhaps
not perfectly inarticulate,
yet I am sure none tells any of the others,
"We are examples of one thing,
we are harmonious instances,
we are inevitably in love."

Sometimes, possibly always, you and I
are performing our lives at considerable
distances. I will admit that very often
I find myself yearning toward my typewriter
or my telephone. Instead I let the hurt
or tender places soothe themselves
in their own specifics, balms of the body
that bears and will bury them.

There are things we do not need
to tell each other. But—our names,
we have told each other our names,
and that pain will not quite heal.

SCHERZO

Jack said I heard
dreams are to keep us asleep
because if we had to respond
directly to our needs we'd have to wake
up and Jill said
you mean dreams let us keep our responses
symbolic and Jack said
yeah.

So Jill said think
of this then if you are hip to paradox
dreams get longer and more detailed
close to morning as if they
are fitting us to the world
we wake to.

Jack said okay then
dreams are like life itself
working on the one hand to keep
us alive and on the other to make
us ready for death.

For the return to
the elements Jill agreed
so why don't you get out of that
sleeping bag and get us some water.

THE PASSIONATE SHEPHERD TO HIS LOVE

"When I was a boy
I wanted more than anything
to become a priest.

"I would sit silently
and full of awe in empty churches
and imagine myself intoning the Mass.

                          I could imagine the little bells,
                          the murmur of
                          the congregation.

"And then I met you
and found how powerful the body can be
in its war with the spirit.

"And of course you know
I am not sorry, or I wouldn't
be talking this way:

                          sometimes when you are lying
                          naked on our bed I look at you
                          and imagine the little bells,
                          the murmur of all those lonely men
                          and women
                          telling their strings of dark beads."

THE FEARS OF RUNNING BEAR

"Even more than I grieve for my nation,
for what your people had done to
all the former nations, large or small,
friendly or hostile to my own people;
even more than I still feel storms of alarm
when I look at your white eyes
which the Iroquois fathers had predicted;
even more than I weep in my heart
to see how you have driven the gods
out of the land and must make things
and sell things rather than have them
come willingly, fairly, and properly
into your hands or justly elude you;
even more than all of these things
I am afraid of the ways that you think.

"Your religions, your tales, your strategies
talk always of three, seven, or ten:
even your children you teach in their stories
to revere things which come in threes,
not in twos or in fours. And I wonder
to myself, 'In fact what kinds of creatures *do*
come in threes?' I do not know them.
And you—do you not know male and female,
the two eyes and arms, and all the twos
of an animal? I fear people who do not
know east and west, or the four faces
of a man, front and back, right and left.
More than anything in this life I fear
a person who does not know what he is."

GOING TO WORK FOR HORACE SONDERGARD

To be precisely accurate
what you will be required to do
in this position is
to be precisely accurate.

This includes
being punctual,
dressing modestly,
and having some respect for your fingernails.

The man to whom you will be
directly responsible
is Horace Sondergard.
He lisps and does not like
being ridiculed. Nor does his wife,
who is hideous.

Your salary will be commensurate
with your ability to put up with
this sort of thing.

I myself am not very well paid
but I find that being able to laugh
at these fucking maniacs
is more gratifying than
owning an expensive car.

ALL ANGELS ARE TERRIBLE

"They are beautiful and quiet.
Sometimes I imagine that one
asks me to come to his bed.
Because he is alone
and has been alone
in an old building
since before any of us was born."

       "Would you go, then?
       Would you sleep with this gothic
       figure who would show you through
       the large rooms and at last
       invite you to the swollen tower?"

"If I could believe he was real
perhaps I would go. I would have to sort
him out among the dark wooden pillars
and the tall chairs. But he would not ask me.
His voice is unimaginable. Its tenor
would be absorbed by the tapestries
and the rich carpets of the stairways.
Whatever he said to me would come from
too many directions—from the myriad leaded lights
at the tops of the windows, from the gilt
triptych, the brass censers, the portraits
with alarming eyes."

       And you would lie naked,
       alabaster, alone in the center
       of the great hall: in all of that
       age and richness and darkness
       the only white object."

"A living flesh. Yes.
Innocent in its proper place."

RUBY CHURCH

She don't look
like much, I mean
she ain't handsome
with her flat brown
face, and people have been known
to hint she's stupid. But if
I was you I wouldn't hurry
to make up my mind about that.

It was around four
in the afternoon and the sky
was green clouds. Over there
was black and there was a lot
of sheet lightnin'. No thunder.
No wind, even. Just weird silence
and it was god-awful hot.

All of a sudden we seen it
sort of flop down outta the sky
like a horse's pecker and then
in just a couple seconds it was the biggest
goddamned busiest tornado ever come through here
headin' for Ruby's house which ain't
nothin' but a shack anyhow. Or wasn't.

It blew that little house apart
like dynamite goin' off in a picnic-basket,
and we run over there half crazy
for fear we would see somethin' awful,
like chunks of Ruby Church and plenty
of blood and that kind of mess.

Instead we seen Ruby Church
just settin' in the middle of her floor,

which was exactly all that was left
of her house. Anderson said, "Ruby,
you're crazy as hell and six times
as lucky" (which I recollect perfect
due to how it made me laugh),
and Ruby said no, yer in the middle
of things and you always got to remember that.
She said when she seen the tornado
comin', or maybe heard it first, she
just made herself remember how
yer always in the middle of things,
or should be—and so she set as close
to the middle of that house as she could
figger out and she just concentrated
on bein' in the middle of everything
in the whole goddamned world, or so
she says, and she was still thinkin' about it
when we come runnin' up.